Missouri

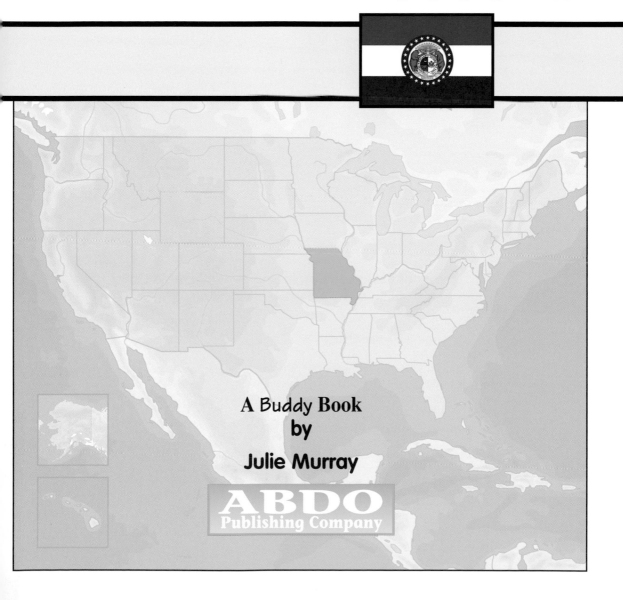

A Buddy Book
by
Julie Murray

ABDO
Publishing Company

VISIT US AT
www.abdopub.com

Published by ABDO Publishing Company, 4940 Viking Drive, Edina, Minnesota 55435.

Copyright © 2006 by Abdo Consulting Group, Inc. International copyrights reserved in all countries. No part of this book may be reproduced in any form without written permission from the publisher. Buddy Books™ is a trademark and logo of ABDO Publishing Company.

Printed in the United States.

Edited by: Sarah Tieck
Contributing Editor: Michael P. Goecke
Graphic Design: Deb Coldiron, Maria Hosley
Image Research: Sarah Tieck
Photographs: Clipart.com, Corbis, Digital Vision, John Foxx Photos, Library of Congress, One Mile Up, PhotoDisc

Library of Congress Cataloging-in-Publication Data

Murray, Julie, 1969-
    Missouri / Julie Murray.
        p. cm. — (The United States)
    Includes index.
        Contents: A snapshot of Missouri — Where is Missouri? — All about Missouri — Cities and the capital — Famous citizens — Gateway Arch — Missouri's caves — Mark Twain National Forest — A history of Missouri.
        ISBN 1-59197-684-7
            1. Missouri—Juvenile literature. I. Title.

F466.3.M87 2006
977.8—dc22

                                                                2005041204

Table Of Contents

A Snapshot Of Missouri

The state of Missouri is located where the Missouri River meets the Mississippi River. These two rivers are the longest in North America.

Many products are shipped on these rivers. This gives Missouri an important role in the United States.

Missouri even got its name from the Missouri River. It is a Native American word meaning "town of the large canoes."

A barge on the
Mississippi River.

There are 50 states in the United States. Every state is different. Each state has an official nickname. Missouri is sometimes called the "Show Me State." Many people say this came from an 1899 speech by a congressman named Willard Duncan Vandiver. He said, "I am from Missouri. You have got to show me."

Missouri became the 24th state on August 10th, 1821. Today, Missouri is the 19th-largest state in the United States. It has 69,709 square miles (180,545 sq km) of land. It is home to 5,595,211 people.

A view of the Mississippi River
near the city of Hannibal.

Where Is Missouri?

There are four parts of the United States. Each part is called a region. Each region is in a different area of the country. The United States Census Bureau says the four regions are the Northeast, the South, the Midwest, and the West.

Missouri is in the Midwest region of the United States. Missouri has four seasons. These seasons are spring, summer, fall, and winter.

Four Regions of the United States of America

ALASKA

WASHINGTON
MONTANA
NORTH DAKOTA
MINNESOTA
VERMONT
MAINE
OREGON
IDAHO
WYOMING
SOUTH DAKOTA
WISCONSIN
MICHIGAN
NEW HAMPSHIRE
MASSACHUSETTS
NEW YORK
RHODE ISLAND
CONNECTICUT
NEVADA
UTAH
COLORADO
NEBRASKA
IOWA
ILLINOIS
INDIANA
OHIO
PENNSYLVANIA
NEW JERSEY
DELAWARE
Washington D.C.
MARYLAND
CALIFORNIA
KANSAS
MISSOURI
WEST VIRGINIA
VIRGINIA
KENTUCKY
NORTH CAROLINA
ARIZONA
NEW MEXICO
OKLAHOMA
ARKANSAS
TENNESSEE
SOUTH CAROLINA
TEXAS
MISSISSIPPI
ALABAMA
GEORGIA
LOUISIANA
FLORIDA

HAWAII

West   Midwest   South   Northeast

Missouri has warm weather
in the spring and summer.

Missouri is bordered by eight other states and a river. Iowa lies to the north. Oklahoma, Kansas, and Nebraska lie to the west. Arkansas is Missouri's neighbor to the south. Illinois, Kentucky, and Tennessee are to the east. The Mississippi River makes up Missouri's eastern border, too.

Missouri

State abbreviation: MO

State nickname: Show Me State

State capital: Jefferson City

State motto: *Salus populi suprema lex esto* (Latin for "The Welfare of the People Be the Supreme Law")

Statehood: August 10, 1821, 24th state

Population: 5,595,211, ranks 17th

State flag: Adopted in 1913

Land area: 69,709 square miles (180,545 sq km), ranks 19th

State tree: Flowering dogwood

State song: "Missouri Waltz"

State government: Three branches: legislative, executive, and judicial

Average July temperature: 78°F (26°C)

Average January temperature: 30°F (-1°C)

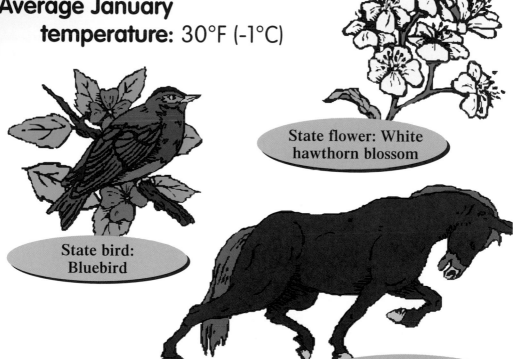

State flower: White hawthorn blossom

State bird: Bluebird

State animal: Missouri mule

Cities And The Capital

Kansas City is the largest city in Missouri. It is located on Missouri's border, near the state of Kansas. Kansas City is known as the "City of Fountains." No one knows exactly how many fountains are in Kansas City. Some say the only city with more fountains is Rome, Italy.

The skyline of Kansas City.

St. Louis is Missouri's second-largest city. It is home to the Gateway Arch. The Gateway Arch is one of the most popular tourist attractions in Missouri. Many people also visit Forest Park. The St. Louis Art Museum, the St. Louis Zoo, the St. Louis Science Center, and the Missouri Historical Society are all located in this city park.

The **capital** of Missouri is Jefferson City. Jefferson City was named after President Thomas Jefferson. It is located in the middle of the state. It is on the banks of the Missouri River.

The skyline of St. Louis at night.

Famous Citizens

Harry S. Truman (1884–1972)

Harry S. Truman

Harry S. Truman was born in Lamar in 1884. He was president of the United States from 1945 to 1953. He was the 33rd president of the United States. Truman is remembered as one of the most important presidents. This is because he took over when President Franklin D. Roosevelt died in 1945. This was important because the United States was fighting in World War II. Truman was also president during the Korean War in the 1950s.

Famous Citizens

Mark Twain (1835–1910)

Mark Twain was named Samuel Clemens when he was born in Florida, Missouri. The name Mark Twain is a pen name. Twain was a famous author and humorist. He wrote books about life on and around the Mississippi River. His most famous books are *The Adventures of Huckleberry Finn* and *The Adventures of Tom Sawyer*.

Mark Twain

Gateway Arch

Many people travel to St. Louis to ride a tram to the top of the Gateway Arch. There is a tram in each hollow leg of the Arch. Both trams have eight cars. It takes about four minutes for the ride each way.

The view from the observation room at the top of the Gateway Arch is spectacular. At the top, there are windows with a view of the city of St. Louis and of western Illinois. On a clear day, it is possible to see 30 miles (48 km).

The Gateway Arch's shadow falls over St. Louis.

The Gateway Arch sits on the banks of the Mississippi River in St. Louis. It is 630 feet (192 m) high. It is taller than the Statue of Liberty and the Washington Monument.

The Gateway Arch got its name from pioneers who crossed the Mississippi River at St. Louis. They were headed west. Back then, the western part of the United States was a great wilderness. St. Louis was on the way, so the area became known as the "Gateway to the West."

A view of the Gateway Arch.

Missouri's Caves

Missouri has more than 5,600 caves. Some of the caves are millions of years old.

Rock formations such as stalagmites and stalactites are found inside the caves. Stalactites hang from the ceilings of caves. They look like giant icicles. Stalagmites form on cave floors. Stalactites and stalagmites are created when minerals build up on the cave surfaces over time.

Stalactites on the ceiling of a cave.

Meramec Caverns is one famous cave system in Missouri. It has many caves to explore. These caves also have a long history. Some say escaped slaves hid in caves on their way to freedom. Other stories say that famous outlaws such as Jesse James used the caves as a hideout from the law.

Mark Twain National Forest

Mark Twain National Forest is the only national forest in Missouri. The forest covers about 1.5 million acres (600,000 ha) of land. It is located in the southern and central parts of the state.

The forest is part of the Ozark Mountains. Its landscape includes limestone mountains, valleys, and streams. Animals and wildflowers also live in this national forest.

Mark Twain National Forest is part
of the Ozark Mountains.

Mark Twain National Forest offers a variety of outdoor activities. Hiking, biking, camping, fishing, and horseback riding are among the popular activities there.

Missouri

1673: French explorers Jacques Marquette and Louis Jolliet explore the Mississippi River.

1764: The city of St. Louis is founded by French fur traders.

1803: President Thomas Jefferson arranges for the United States to buy Missouri as part of the Louisiana Purchase.

1804: Meriwether Lewis and William Clark explore America. They start their journey near St. Louis at Camp Dubois.

1821: Missouri becomes the 24th state on August 10.

1860: The first pony express delivery riders leave St. Joseph.

A pony express rider.

1904: St. Louis hosts the World's Fair. This celebrates the 100th anniversary of the **Louisiana Purchase**.

The "Biggest Wheel on Earth" was at the World's Fair in St. Louis.

1945: Harry S. Truman of Lamar becomes the president of the United States.

1965: The Gateway Arch is completed in St. Louis.

1993: Missouri experiences floods along the Mississippi River.

2000: Missouri governor Mel Carnahan dies in a plane crash.

2001: John Ashcroft of Springfield is appointed Attorney General of the United States.

2004: The St. Louis Cardinals baseball team makes it to the World Series. They are defeated by the Boston Red Sox who win for the first time since 1918.

Cities In Missouri

St. Joseph

Hannibal

Florida

Independence

Kansas City

Jefferson City ★

St. Louis

Lamar

Springfield

Important Words

capital a city where government leaders meet.

Louisiana Purchase a deal where the United States bought land from France. Part of this land later became Missouri.

nickname a name that describes something special about a person or a place.

outlaw a person who is being hunted by the police for breaking the law.

pioneers people who traveled across the United States in the 1800s to settle the western United States.

slave a person who is bought and sold as property.

wilderness wild, unsettled land.

World War II the second war between many countries, which happened from 1939 to 1945.

Web Sites

To learn more about Missouri, visit ABDO Publishing Company on the World Wide Web. Web site links about Missouri are featured on our Book Links page. These links are routinely monitored and updated to provide the most current information available.

www.abdopub.com

Index